Another Life

Eulalia Books
300 Fraser Purchase Road
Latrobe, PA 15650

hello@eulaliabooks.com

Michelle Gil-Montero and Román Antopolsky, Editors
Tyler Friend, Designer

Cover image: Román Antopolsky

ISBN: 978-1-7329363-6-2

Eulalia Books is affiliated with the School of Arts, Humanities, and Social Sciences at Saint Vincent College.

Another

Life

Daniel Lipara

Translated by Robin Myers

Eulalia Books 2021

Contents

My aunt Susana weighs three hundred thirty pounds
my mother's eldest sister
who wears bright muumuus printed tunics
who keeps her hair cut short with highlights paints shadow
   on her eyes
and rarely leaves the house
her house that smells of sandalwood two computers
murmuring like wind and night
my aunt never had pets or children
lives off her father the son
of a butcher who fled the pogroms all the way to Argentina

Susana
which means beautiful as a lotus flower

she had two knee replacements
and then was hospitalized for her weight
it didn't slim her down her bones kept straining
they shrank her stomach with a belt the belt snapped open
   scratched her innards
food crept up to her lungs
but even so the ice cream flutters down inside her
gold-papered chocolates tumbling like black snow

Susana
which means beautiful as a lotus flower

who's never without angels
she buys angel stickers in bulk

from stores in the Once neighborhood and gives them away
   she says god listens to me
but her boyfriend Héctor lost weight and left
her husband Aarón ran off with a man
and her sister my mother has cancer
she'll be up in the soaring stars someday
like an angel

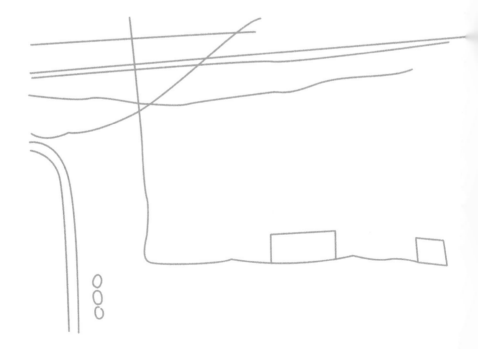

My father's name is Jorge
proud man with long black hair his shirt unbuttoned on his
   chest
son of Francisco the Italian charterer
he lives in Mataderos
where the air smells of slaughtered cows
his surname is the island of Aeolus his first name he who
   tills the soil
he drives a cab
my mother hailed it fleeing her first husband
then I was born then Nadia
which means hope

his black dog
darted in the background
and hunted pigeons out behind my grandfather's lemon tree
he trailed me let me clutch his fur that's how I learned to walk
his name was Prometheus
old shepherd he'd wag his tail at the sight of my father
he couldn't run to him his hind legs faltered
and darkness hunted him
behind the lemon tree

master griller
he taught me how to build a fire
with branches eucalyptus leaves bark shavings
the air snaps
we burn the meat fling entrails to the flames of leafless logs

universality of collective consciousness

and gusts of smoke bluster the grease into the sky
I'm six years old
we drive home as the evening
fills my eyes with sleep
the sky with stars

his father burned my father's books
on this same grill
war broke out but he wasn't called to fight
he drove a truck down south he had his Minotaur radio
and now Francisco's dead his life
dashed off like wind

Jorge fought at home
sometimes he comes back and sleeps with my mother
the house smells of grilled meat like Aeolus's island
and after the feast he washes down with wine
he roots around under the hood of the Taunus his hands slick
he pulls out parts and tubes and cables
and washes all that metal
like a hunter
who slits the belly of a wild boar
to draw its guts out gently trying not to scrape them
divides the lungs from heart from liver
and cleans the inside of the body

Lipari island

boundaries of the line

A walled-in island
a craggy shore is where Ulysses docked at last in his black
   ships
it's the home of Aeolus the god beloved by the gods the god
   of wind
who lives with all his children feasting on ambrosia
Aeolus and six sons six daughters married to each other
his house smells of grilled meat

the island is named
after the king
who founds the city and begins to work the land the king
   who tills
they built the early houses out of lava people say
he's Aeolus's son they say he's the grandson
of Ulysses and Calypso

besieged and plundered
the island is abandoned is a desert of obsidian
adrift in wine-dark seas until the first Doric Greeks arrive
who stave off their assailants the Etruscan pirates
and form a mighty fleet
and are also pirates

Diodorus Siculus in his Bibliotheca Historica calls
the island of the Liparesi small but singularly fertile
it has the riches needed for a lavish life
like fish of every species all those trees

mythic temporality
x lived temporality

language as origin

13

laden with sumptuous fruits
that offer myriad delights

prosperous city of the Roman Empire
famed for its fleet and for obsidian black stone of halted lava
it's a land of exile too
and haven for ascetic monks
and bishopric the Ostrogoths invade
the Byzantines reoccupy

and now Monte Pelato
erupts
the island is despoiled by Muslim pirates
who murder every man and kidnap every woman
deserted for two hundred years
it's silent now

the Normans come
and give Lipari to black monks
the farmers tame their lands
those cast-off lands
now theirs by order of the abbot
and by the Angevins and Aragón

two hundred ships
burn the cathedral set every house ablaze
enslave the men and women the ships
of Barbarrosa the cruel
the island is deserted all the fruit trees razed it is
a land of ash and ember

Liliana, lily blossom

My mother's five-foot nine
she has big bones and bleach blonde hair
white crinkle cotton dresses on milky blue-veined skin
skin sweet with perfume
and draped with necklaces she wears at home
our house of grass-green carpets our house without flowers
in Once where our neighbors' heads are covered
because god's up there above it all
though I'm not sure about my mother's god

her name is Liliana
which means beautiful as a lily blossom

her grandmothers Fanny and Zelda were sisters
they could read the future in coffee grounds
and they knew everything about you from your birthday
    they were famous
they traveled far their customers were high-ranked officers
    important people
they hoped my mother would inherit their gift
but she's a therapist
receives her clients in the living room
and sees things sometimes
sometimes at night she flings my covers off like something's
    wrong
and sometimes she walks backwards
like something's wrong

Liliana
lily blossom

my mother left Gerardo her first husband
she fled at night these things happen at night
she took the first black cab she saw
it was my father the tiller Aeolus led him
I was already in her belly when they married they named
    me Daniel
but in the end my father left a knife clutched in my mother's
    hand
and now her parents coax her to remarry they want her
    house to have a man in it again
Ricardo her latest boyfriend's not around we don't know why
he lives in Avellaneda
he's a blacksmith

like the lily
Liliana

we live
many lives she says
our souls are old or damp and cool as flowers
and when you die god thrusts your head into the river
and you forget it all
you're light in the sky in the stars
in an orchard circled by hedges stately trees
pear and apple and fig trees their branches always heavy
and apple follows apple and pear follows pear
each yields to the other
delicious fruits

that offer myriad delights
and god thrusts your head into the river
you come back as a tree
an animal

I'm eleven
I'm drinking orange juice with my mother in a coffee shop
I think I won't remember her
won't recognize her if I see her in another life
don't be like that souls travel as a group yes even in the stars
they change I might become your grandson or your cousin
   imagine that
a dog you have a spider in its web
a flower blooming on the terrace

Liliana
like a lily blossom

Estela morning star
is a friend of my mother's she lives in San Miguel
her street is lined with palm trees she has dogs and chickens
she cleanses
my mother's energy
and lays her hands onto my mother's vengeful cells
and reads the planets
as my sister and I play with the dogs
and she says
my father will come back
come back from Ciudad Oculta the land of exile where he
   lives
with Analía she who never rests

that barren land that isn't his
so now on Sundays
my mother calls Jorge we visit monks
and go to Rosario to see Ignacio the priest born in Ceylon
    and father Mario in González Catán
and the universal church of the kingdom of god
where the pastor leads you up to the altar
and the evil spirits disappear

Sai Baba

A cobra
in the bedsheets of the boy
among palm fields and rice fields
the soundless cobra with the cosmos printed on its neck
the king of snakes
curls in the cradle of Sathya Narayana Rayu
the son of farmers
in a town of stone and straw in Puttaparthi

he speaks to animals
to pigs and zebus to the rats and dogs running in the field
one day he faints into a ditch what bit him
he's different when he wakes
he sings in Sanskrit now sometimes he laughs or weeps out
    of the blue
he talks about fruit trees that no one's ever seen
and calls for rites because the gods he says
are moving through the sky right now

an exorcist
slaughters a pheasant and a lamb
he sits him down and draws a ring of blood around him
    in the field
he shaves his head he slashes him
and cleans his wounds
with lemon juice and garlic but Rayu won't speak
his father is afraid he grabs a stick he screams you're crazy
you're either a ghost or a god

one morning
he gets up and calls for his family
he gives them fruits and flowers he pulls out of the blue and
   he says
I'm the reincarnation
of the holy Muslim fakhir
my lineage and my clan are sacred I am
Sai Baba
divine father divine mother

Susana speaks

Every tree has a soul
and so do cars and furniture
drive carefully I tell the taxi drivers the car is suffering
if I'm depressed my TV set shuts off and won't turn on again
until I'm better and it comes back on all by itself
and sometimes I forget
that I have access to the cosmos
to my grandmothers with their tea and chatter among the
    fruit trees
one night I dreamed I took a cab through Once to buy
    something
I even remember the streets

and when I went the next morning I thought
there's going to be a house with decorations who knows
    where I'll be sent
they were stickers
the clerk told me I dreamed you came
I dreamed I sold a fat woman some angels
that's why I'm giving them to you
so you'll remember
that the cosmos wants you to ask it for everything the cosmos
    wants
you to ask blindly don't hold back that drives
it crazy

it's a gift in this family
a gift from my grandmothers Fanny and Zelda

who were sisters you're the grandson and cousin of your
    grandfather the son and cousin of your mother
we're descendants of an old Russian seer
people would travel from all over for the chance to meet him
our family is connected to the cosmos
I know that Héctor is the reincarnation of a sorcerer
Aarón and I have made a pact
that whichever one of us is first to go will send
a sign

we talked the other day
your mom and I
I told her how I was an Arab sheikh and a Greek priestess
    in another life
she says tell me about the priestess
I say so what I saw is that I'm on a hillside wearing a
    white tunic
and then my mother interrupts her and she says we're in
    the hills
with water and volcanoes all around us the wind's blowing
    in the house of the gods
the men are tilling in the valley
the grease spits skyward in its gusts of smoke
Susana we were there together

she speaks and burns
sandalwood incense on a plate
my aunt beautiful as a lotus flower
she says I dreamed we went to India and your mother was
    healed
the smoke thread opens like a cobra's neck

Sai Baba hanging on the wall he wasn't there before
he looks straight at the bed
across the grass-green carpet
my mother says yes Susana gets a map and says here look
her finger moves across the sea to India

if Jorge the tiller were to come to Ezeiza Airport

Where
are Liliana's arms
the white arms of my children says my father the tiller
he drove to Ezeiza in his black car
and searched until he found us sitting on our luggage
with my aunt and my mother waiting for
the flight to India
he took my hand my sister's hand
what if something happens to you what would I do then
I'd crash the taxi turn to dust let the wind blow me away
and let my bones drift down to earth
I have no parents
Susana can go alone let her go see
Sai Baba let her travel to that tusk
suspended from the earth
over the black waters of the Indian Ocean
and now my sister spreads her arms wants him to pick her up
she's frightened by the airport's metal voice
my father laughs kisses her hair again and again
he shifts my sister to my mother's arms my mother laughs
    and cries
lily blossom Liliana
she checks the screen
dark as the ocean floor
it's boarding now Jorge it's just a month
she touches the face
of my father he who tills the land who never plowed the skies
and who shows us the way

like puppies in a field
of wandering leaves
dispersed by wind

imaginative act of
one situation
has ripple effects
into other myths

myth & memory

— how does memory form myth
— places & people
   overlapping

myth becoming an ideal
   resistant to reality

Everyone's asleep
as the vessel moves across the sea at night
and I
don't know where I'm going or
what lonely stretch of water lies below
this South African Airways Airbus A320
the vessel where everyone sleeps
as the night and the ocean are the same

the air is simple darkness
and my mother and my sister
dream is dreaming different if
your head is flying at six hundred miles an hour surrounded
  by air
and stars that spin and sound like engines
like a note ringing loud and clear
in the ears of the night

I don't know where I'm going
Johannesburg New Delhi Bangalore Puttaparthi
I know the sea is down below
I saw it as the sun sank
veiled with shadow six hundred miles beneath
the gentle vessel
where sleep is light as fire
where clouds are born and wind and snow

and space shrills in our ears
like a mosquito

It was dark
and I watched the sun rise through the windows at Indira
   Gandhi Airport
the planes rest in the fog
the orange Delhi light I'm here
the Air India 803 brings us to Bangalore the garden city
I plow the sky
fly over the land of Sai Baba
just hours from his ashram Prasanthi Nilayam the house of
   highest peace
last flight and rice no meat to grill out here
the sacred cows
are gifts from a goddess who nurses her children
sacred as tigers monkeys cobras elephants
the vessel trembles there are wells of air my aunt says
   maybe it's the gods
moving through the sky right now
we take a cab
from Bangalore to Puttaparthi over broken roads
one hundred and twenty-five miles across the Karnataka
   plains
the slopes of Andhra Pradesh
over baked earth
earth strewn with stones
as if a mountainside had shattered
dry thatched-roof villages
with trees for shade
where oxen and zebus wander across the road

water buffalo plow the rice fields
boys herd and women walk with jugs of water
beneath a raging sun
my aunt speaks English to the driver
the car turns at the granite mountains where the road
   constricts
and climbs the hills we're close
Susana says look that's a hospital an airport Baba built it
   all of it
to lead us
from the shadows to the light

Puttaparthi, "land of anthills"

And we descend
to the land of the ants
angels hang from the entry arch
the car follows the sandy road into the valley's heart
where the air thickens with the hum of rickshaws and
    motorcycles
the air that smells of fruit and earth
and Baba's everywhere he hangs above
cows sleeping in the shade
above the beggars and the women dressed in pink and
    sky-blue cloth
we watch it all
like deer who dart across an open field
and then halt something's there

Susana translates

the man says
the village used to be called
Gollapalli home of the cattle herders
and all the fields were full of beautiful fat cows
and once a herder
worried because his favorite wasn't giving any milk
found her suckling a cobra
he flew into a rage and seized a rock and crushed the snake
    and she
wheezing her dying breath
released a curse and now the earth she said
shall be an anthill

and the car turned
and we drove through the gate of the ashram
the gardens
where the gods are still
his skin is blue his head a monkey's or an elephant's
the worshipers dressed in white kurtas
with little flags around their necks
sing ohm beneath the flaming trees
they're waiting for the darshan to begin the vision of god
where Baba will appear

those boys
follow the car they want to take our luggage
for a few rupees they want
to bring them upstairs to this room two beds two mattresses
we've rented in the ashram
they're going to make an exception Susana says
so you can sleep here because men and women sleep
and eat and pray apart
and I
I'll have to learn
to eat as silently as plants
go ceremoniously to the mandir
ask Sai Baba to heal my mother ask
with a grave stream of silence

Liliana
lily blossom brings a coconut
brimming with water that's nutritious as a steak she says
see that's the man who sells them cuts them open with a
    machete

now I
am also dressed in white
with a small Argentine flag on my back
a dot of ash between my eyes
burned cow dung ash and milk ash of the cosmos vibhuti
as the sun sinks and veils the roads
and further back the hills of Anantapur the ashen sea and
   further still
my house
my father the tiller

3 a.m.
the alarm goes off
I slip out silently so I
won't wake my mother at this hour
when sleep still nestles in her head
and in the heads of birds
I know how to get to the temple and I know the gods
still as fig trees along the path
bound to the world with roots
no lights are on in Baba's house
the phone booth's closed the canteen where I eat alone
the sound of crickets
and my strange crackling steps
crumple the silence
and the distance though there are others now
all dressed in white sitting in rows and waiting for the
  mandir doors
to open
hours from now
my mother says I get up early
so god will hear me first
but what I like is one leg crossed over the other
the tingling in my hands my arm asleep
as the birds wake
and the day glows all over
and everything's so calm I almost don't know why
I'm here
an ant in the sequence of ants

the doors open
with the first ray of sun
we file into the temple we're led to sing to call to god
five ohms through the nose eyes ears skin and tongue
through the feet anus penis hands and throat
through the air that lives inside the body
through what enfolds the body
and one last ohm for me
shanti shanti shanti

this is what speaks when no one speaks

what does it sound like
the jug of the mind
a rivulet of rain of birdsong
that twig of meaning at the border of my bowl in the canteen
and if I move
and if I walk up to the current
it's the rustle of flowers the stone that breaks the surface of
   the water
the name as brilliant as a clearing in the woods of noise
or more concretely an American
who speaks a phrase almost in Spanish

this is what speaks when no one speaks

when my mother tripped on a mound of dirt
and wrenched her foot
we took a rickshaw she exposed her swollen ankle
and the man brought us to the clinic
the waiting room is full
we're the only ones dressed in white people come up to us
they look concerned about my mother
they speak in Hindi in Sanskrit what is it they speak
to become this oracle
who answers a question
that I don't want to ask myself that no one asked

origin of language
& silence

35

this is what speaks when no one speaks

I was in the mandir
waiting for Baba to come out the sun had risen
and then a language spoke to me
coarse as the voice
that turned into a tree and still has lips
the old man with ebony skin
no flag around his neck
drew in a long thin thread of breath blew out a tiny ball
   without an aftertaste
and looked at me as if to say it's your turn now
forget about what brought you here
your school your friends the girl you like your other life

this is what speaks when no one speaks

and the fingers of the day wake up the sky
and wash its eyes of fog
and everyone moves toward the temple doors they want to
    get there first
like the wind
when it brings the murmur of the waves all dressed in white
who rise and hurry to the shore
with open mouths

and that baby monkey
my sister inches toward it
she wants to touch that fur with her own hands
and now out of the blue the mother monkey's here she
    howls and grabs my sister's clothes and hair
she's furious
more monkeys come down from the trees
surround my sister

like lava lighting up
a monkey in the jungle
that's how the faithful show themselves
to god

and the man filling bags with ashes
under the eaves shaped like an insect wing
he shovels cosmic ash
into each bag
beneath an insect wing

like crickets singing to the night
huddled in nothingness
in a force field of sound
that's what mantras are like
like crickets
everywhere

and what would my father
the tiller say
if he could see me sitting here alone
eating rice
wearing a white kurta

like a cage in god's garden
that banyan fig
with aerial roots growing downward from the branches
to drive into the ground
in the garden of god

and I heard
the bird
circling
over a long ohm
its little bird claws
scratching it

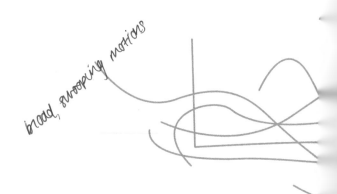

broad, swooping motions

like the spider
turning its prey around
and around engulfing it in thread
that's how the tailor wraps my mother in a sari
like the spider

the goddess looks at me
from her glass box
with all her heads
five heads stuck to each other
she trails me with her open
eyes as I make my way to the temple
at three in the morning

like those black ants appearing
out of the blue taking away
the wandering leaves dispersed by wind
that's how rickshaws appear and take us away
like ants

and that woman
who offered me
brown and white bits of coconut
as I drifted through the ashram alone
near the waterfall
the coconut woman

and the gods are there watching us
and the gods are there watching us

the washerwomen
I saw when I climbed the hill
they shine all dressed in white in the valley washing white
   sheets
the water shining
between the green fields the hills

all day
my voice hid in my throat
like a mouse
in a dresser
a knot of silence in my throat

like ghosts
those glints of tooth and hair
the girls from school
I jacked off thinking of them when I was supposed to nap
it's been a long time since I've seen them and now
they're glints of tooth and hair

it was still dark
I sat down on my folding chair
and waited for the temple doors to open
and now it's day
I sing and call to god
he comes

the head dipping into the river
in this orchard of fruit trees
of flowers and birds with no name
cows resting in the shade
my father's Taunus
newly washed the engine running
is this what sacred means
the burned dung ash streaked on my forehead
the vessel moving across the night
the gods hiding in the fields
the smell of livestock in the afternoon in Mataderos
my mother
coming toward me like a dog a spider in another life
the heads of god that watch me
Sai Baba dressed in orange making something manifest
the island of Aeolus
where Ulysses disembarked where my grandfather was born
and washerwomen shining in the valley with their sheets
my nine-year-old sister in her white kurta
and the monkey who pulls her hair
is this what sacred means
the coconut just cut down from the tree
my aunt with all her angels
the cabs the maps the boys hauling luggage
the footsteps of the gods across the sky
is all of this what sacred means
my mother's cancer
(this lineage of leaves the wind disperses and returns)
the smoke from the meat
the engines rumbling like stars

It's over
the plane is down below and clouds of smoke
rise from the ground and step into the house of the gods
where the air echoes into the wind and stars
we drop lower
the vessel moves across the cloudfloor
over the river islands streams that slip into the fields
this wooded land that would be empty
if it weren't tilled
and because the noise picks up and I drop lower
and the air presses harder in my ears
the dense sound of this journey from another life
because I'm home again because the plane
is touching down to earth

attempting
to draw
something
not usual

resistance to closure

what is driving the collection?
. engaging w an epic
. absence of closure - too much?
if this is a deliberate gesture,
  what is that gesture?

colophon

This book was finished on January 24, 2018.

Liliana lily blossom died on November 1, 2000.

Jorge the tiller died on May 28, 2016.

Susana lotus flower still listens to the footsteps of the gods
in the sky and buys angels in Once.

Mi tía pesa ciento cincuenta kilos
la hermana mayor de mi madre
que usa grandes camisolas de color túnicas estampadas
el pelo corto con reflejos y en los ojos sombra
y sale poco de su casa
de su casa de olor a sándalo dos computadoras
que sueltan un rumor de viento y noche
mi tía nunca tuvo hijos ni animales
vive de su padre el hijo
de un carnicero que llegó al país huyendo de los pogroms

se llama Susana
que significa bella como flor de loto

le operaron las rodillas
y se internó por sobrepeso
no adelgazó sus huesos siguieron cargando
le acortaron el estómago con un cinturón el cinturón se
   abrió rasgó por dentro
la comida llegó hasta el pulmón
pero igual el helado cae nevando en su interior
bombones de papel dorado caen como copos negros

Susana
que significa bella como flor de loto

y siempre tiene ángeles
calcomanias con ángeles que compra

al por mayor en Once y los regala porque dice dios me
   escucha
pero su novio Héctor adelgazó y se fue
Aarón su esposo se fue con un hombre
y su hermana mi madre tiene cáncer
va a estar en las altas estrellas
como un ángel

Jorge es el nombre de mi padre
hombre orgulloso de negro pelo largo la camisa abierta
    sobre el pecho
hijo de Francisco el fletero italiano
vive en Mataderos
donde el aire huele al sacrificio de las reses
su apellido es la isla de Eolo su nombre el que labra la tierra
maneja un taxi
ahí subió mi madre cuando huía de su primer esposo
después nací yo después Nadia
que es esperanza

su perro negro
corría por el fondo
cazaba palomas atrás del limonero de mi abuelo
me seguía dejaba que me aferrara a su pelo así aprendí a
    caminar
se llamaba Prometeo
viejo pastor veía a mi padre y movía la cola
no podía correr hacia él le fallaban las patas de atrás
lo cazó la oscuridad
bajo el limonero

maestro asador
de él aprendí a hacer el fuego
con hojas de eucalipto ramas trozos de corteza
el aire cruje

quemamos la carne tiramos entrañas al fuego de troncos sin
   hojas
y hasta el cielo sube la grasa en soplos de humo
tengo seis años
volvemos con el auto mientras la tarde
me llena los ojos de sueño
y el cielo de estrellas

su padre le quemó los libros
en la misma parrilla del fondo donde hace el asado
la guerra llegó pero no lo llamaron
fue camionero en el sur tuvo su radio Minotauro
y ahora su padre Francisco está muerto su vida
voló como un viento

Jorge peleó en su casa
a veces vuelve duerme con mi madre
la casa huele a asado como la isla de Eolo
y después del banquete que riega con vino
se mete en el capó del Taunus con las manos engrasadas
saca piezas y cables y caños
lava todo ese metal con agua
como un cazador
cuando abre un jabalí del bosque
y saca las entrañas con cuidado no quiere raspar los intestinos
separa hígado pulmones corazón
y lo limpia por dentro

la isla Lipari

A una isla rodeada de murallas
a una tierra escarpada llegó por fin Ulises con sus naves
    negras
es el hogar de Eolo el dios querido por los dioses dios del
    viento
que vive con sus hijos en banquete rodeado de manjares
Eolo y sus seis hijas y seis hijos casados entre sí
su casa huele a asado

el nombre
de la isla es por el rey
que funda la ciudad y empieza a trabajar la tierra el rey que
    labra
y las primeras casas son de lava dicen
que es el hijo de Eolo y dicen que es el nieto
de Ulises y Calipso

la asedian y saquean
la isla vuelve a estar vacía es un desierto de obsidiana
que flota en el vinoso mar hasta que llegan los primeros
    griegos dóricos
que resisten los ataques de piratas etruscos
y forman una flota poderosa
y también son piratas

Diodoro Sículo en su Bibliotheca Historica
dice la isla de los liparesi es chica pero notablemente fértil
posee todo tipo de productos que hacen que su vida sea
    lujosa
peces de todas las especies y esos árboles

de frutas deliciosas
que ofrecen un deleite extraordinario

de los romanos próspera ciudad imperial
famosa por su flota y la obsidiana piedra negra de la lava fría
también es tierra del exilio
y es refugio de monjes eremitas
y es obispado invaden ostrogodos
la vuelven a ocupar los bizantinos

ahora el Monte Pelato
entra en erupción
la isla es devastada por piratas musulmanes
matan a cada uno de los hombres cada mujer es secuestrada
ahora está en silencio
está vacía por doscientos años

llegan los normandos
y ponen a Lipari en manos de los monjes negros
los labradores se hacen dueños de las tierras que trabajan
esas abandonadas tierras
que son suyas por orden del abad
y de los reyes angevinos y Aragón

doscientas naves
queman la catedral incendian cada casa
hacen esclavos a hombres y mujeres naves
de Barbarroja el cruel
la isla está vacía no hay frutales
es una tierra de ceniza y brasa

Mi madre mide un metro ochenta
tiene los huesos grandes el pelo teñido de rubio
vestidos de bambula blanca sobre la piel blanca con venas
   azules
la piel llena de perfume
llena de collares que usa en casa
nuestra casa de alfombras como pasto casa sin flores
en Once donde todos se cubren la cabeza
porque arriba de todo está dios
aunque no sé si el de mi madre

se llama Liliana
que significa bella como una flor de lirio

sus abuelas Fanny y Zelda eran hermanas
veían el futuro en la borra de café
sabían todo por el día en que naciste eran famosas
viajaban recibían a militares a gente importante
quisieron pasarle a mi madre su don
pero ella es psicóloga
atiende en el living de casa
y a veces ve cosas
a veces a la noche me destapa como si hubiera algo
y a veces camina hacia atrás
como si hubiera algo

Liliana
la flor de lirio

Gerardo su primer esposo
mi madre lo dejó huyó de noche esas cosas pasan de noche
tomó el primer taxi negro que vio
era mi padre el labrador Eolo lo empujaba
se casaron conmigo en el vientre me pusieron Daniel
pero al final mi padre se fue mi madre empuñaba un cuchillo
y ahora sus padres piden que vuelva a casarse que haya un
    hombre en casa
ahora su último novio Ricardo no está no sabemos por qué
vive en Avellaneda
es herrero

como el lirio
Liliana

vivimos
varias vidas dice
las almas son viejas o son húmedas y frescas como flores
y al morir dios te hunde la cabeza en el río
y te olvidás de todo
sos luz en el cielo luz en las estrellas
en un huerto rodeado de setos donde hay árboles grandes
y perales manzanos e higueras siempre están llenas las ramas
la manzana sigue a la manzana la pera a la pera
cada una deja su lugar a otra
frutas deliciosas
que ofrecen un deleite extraordinario
y dios hunde tu cabeza en el río
volvés y sos un árbol
un animal

tengo once años

mi madre y yo desayunamos jugo de naranja en un café

y pienso no voy a acordarme de ella

no voy a darme cuenta si la veo en otra vida

no te pongas así las almas siempre van en grupo aún en las
    estrellas

van cambiando yo puedo ser tu primo tu nieto imaginate

un perro que vos tengas la araña en su tela

una flor que se abre en la terraza

Liliana

como una flor de lirio

estrella de la mañana Estela

es amiga de mi madre vive en San Miguel

donde la calle está llena de palmeras y en su casa hay
    gallinas y perros

y ella lava

la energía de mi madre

y apoya sus manos en las células malignas de mi madre

en el aura en la cabeza pelada en el pecho que falta

y lee los planetas

mientras mi hermana y yo jugamos con los perros

y dice

que mi padre va a volver a casa

volver de Ciudad Oculta tierra del exilio donde vive

con Analía la que no descansa

esa abandonada tierra que no es suya

ahora los domingos

mi madre llama a Jorge vemos a unos monjes

y vamos a Rosario a ver a Ignacio el sacerdote de Ceilán al
    padre Mario en Gonzáles Catán
a la iglesia universal del reino de dios
donde el pastor te lleva hasta el altar
y el demonio se va

Sai Baba

Una cobra
en las sábanas del niño
entre los campos de palmeras y arrozales
la quieta cobra que en su cuello tiene al cosmos
el rey de las serpientes
está en la cuna de Sathya Narayana Rayu
hijo de campesinos
en una aldea de piedra y paja en Puttaparthi

habla a los animales
a los cebúes y a los cerdos a las ratas y los perros del campo
en una acequia cae desmayado un día qué lo picó
cuando despierta es otro
ahora canta en sánscrito a veces ríe o llora de la nada
habla de árboles frutales que no conoce nadie
y pide que hagan ceremonias porque los dioses dice
están pasando ahora por el cielo

un exorcista
mata a un cordero y a un faisán
lo sienta en la mitad del campo traza un círculo de sangre
le rapa la cabeza le hace tajos
lava las heridas
con jugo de limón y ajo pero Rayu no habla
ahora su padre tiene miedo agarra un palo grita sos un loco
sos un dios o un fantasma

una mañana
se levanta y llama a su familia
les da flores y frutas que saca de la nada y dice
soy la reencarnación
del santo faquir musulmán
mi linaje y mi clan son sagrados yo soy
Sai Baba
divino padre divina madre

El árbol tiene alma
tienen los muebles y los autos
les digo a los taxistas que anden con cuidado el auto sufre
si me deprimo se apaga mi televisión y no hay manera
hasta que se me pasa y vuelve sola
me olvido a veces
que tengo línea con el cosmos
con mis abuelas que toman té charlando entre frutales
soñé una vez que me iba en taxi al Once y que compraba
    algo
me acuerdo hasta las calles

y al otro día cuando fui pensé
va a haber una casa de adornos qué sé yo a dónde me
    mandan
eran calcomanías
el empleado dijo soñé que venías
soñé que una gordita me compraba ángeles
por eso los regalo
para hacerte acordar
que el cosmos quiere que le pidas todo el cosmos quiere
que pidas ciegamente sin dudar se desespera
por eso

es don de familia
de mis abuelas Fanny y Zelda
que eran hermanas vos sos nieto y primo de tu abuelo hijo
    y primo de tu madre

venimos de un viejo vidente de Rusia
viajaban desde lejos para verlo
somos familia conectada con el cosmos
yo sé que Héctor es la reencarnación de un hechicero
y con Aarón quedamos
en que el primero en irse le manda al otro
una palabra

recién estábamos
tu madre y yo las dos charlando
le decía que en otra vida fui un jeque árabe y una
     sacerdotisa griega
ella me dijo contame lo de la sacerdotisa
digo lo que vi estoy en el monte vestida con túnica blanca
entonces mi madre la interrumpe y dice estamos en un monte
rodeadas de agua y de volcanes el viento sopla en la casa de
     los dioses
los hombres labran el campo del valle
y hasta el cielo sube la grasa en soplos de humo
estábamos juntas Susana

habla quemando
ramas de sándalo en un plato
mi tía bella como flor de loto
dice soñé que vamos a la India con tu madre y que se cura
el hilo de humo se abre como el cuello de una cobra
Sai Baba cuelga en la pared antes no estaba
mira directo a la cama
sobre la alfombra verde como el pasto
mi madre dice sí Susana trae un mapa y dice acá acá
su dedo cruza el mar hasta la India

si Jorge el labrador viniera a Ezeiza

Dónde están
los brazos de Liliana
los blancos brazos de mis hijos dice mi padre el labrador
llegó hasta Ezeiza en su auto negro
y nos buscó hasta vernos sentados sobre las valijas
con mi tía y mi madre esperando
el avión a la India
a mi hermana y a mí nos agarra las manos
qué voy a hacer si algo les pasa dice
mejor chocar el taxi hacerme polvo que me lleve el viento
y que mis huesos vuelvan a la tierra
padres no tengo
puede ir Susana que ella vaya a ver
a Sai Baba que viaje a ese colmillo
que cuelga de la tierra
sobre las aguas negras del océano Índico
ahora mi hermana abre sus brazos quiere que él la levante
la asusta la metálica voz del aeropuerto
mi padre ríe besa su pelo una y otra vez
pone a mi hermana en brazos de mi madre que ríe y llora
flor de lirio Liliana
consulta la pantalla
oscura como el fondo del océano
es nuestro vuelo Jorge es solo un mes
acaricia la cara
de mi padre el que labra la tierra el que nunca surcó los cielos
y nos muestra el camino
como cachorros en un campo
de hojas errantes
que el viento derrama

Todos duermen
mientras la nave cruza el mar de noche
y yo
no sé a dónde voy
qué solitaria parte de agua
está bajo este Airbus A320 de South African Airways
la nave en la que duermen todos
mientras la noche y el mar son lo mismo

el aire es simple oscuridad
y sueñan
mi madre y mi hermana será distinto el sueño
porque esté la cabeza
volando a mil kilómetros por hora rodeada de aire
de estrellas que giran y suenan a turbinas
a una nota que se hace fuerte
en los oídos de la noche

y yo no sé a dónde voy
Johannesburgo Nueva Delhi Bangalore Puttapartti
sé que abajo está el mar
lo vi mientras el sol caía
la sombra lo velaba diez mil kilómetros abajo
de la nave mullida
donde el sueño es liviano como el fuego
donde nacen las nubes el viento la nieve

y silba el espacio en los oídos
como un mosquito

Era de noche
y vi el amanecer en las ventanas del aeropuerto Gandhi
los aviones descansan en la niebla
en la luz naranja de Nueva Delhi llegué acá
el Air India 803 nos lleva a Bangalore la ciudad jardín
surco el cielo
sobrevuelo la tierra de Sai Baba
a solo horas de su ashram Prasanthi Nilayam la casa de la
    paz suprema
último vuelo arroz acá no hay carne asada
las vacas sagradas
son el regalo de una diosa que da leche a sus hijos
sagradas como los tigres y los monos como la cobra el elefante
la nave tiembla hay pozos de aire pueden ser los dioses dice
    mi tía
que están pasando ahora por el cielo
vamos en taxi
de Bangalore a Puttaparthi por el asfalto roto
doscientos kilómetros por las planicies de Karnataka
y las sierras de Andhra Pradesh
por la árida tierra
la tierra salpicada por las piedras
como si hubiera estallado una montaña
secos poblados con techos de paja
y árboles para la sombra
donde los bueyes y cebúes cruzan el camino
búfalos de agua aran los arrozales
pastorean los chicos hay mujeres con cántaros de agua
bajo la furia del sol

mi tía habla en inglés con el chofer
el auto dobla a las montañas de granito donde el camino
se angosta y trepa las colinas estamos cerca
dice Susana eso de allá es un hospital un aeropuerto todo lo
   hizo Baba todo
para llevarnos
de la sombra a la luz

Puttaparthi, "tierra de hormigueros"

Y bajamos
a la tierra de las hormigas
ángeles cuelgan del arco de entrada
el auto entra al corazón del valle por la calle arenosa
donde el aire se adensa del zumbido de los rickshaws y las
    motos
el aire con olor a fruta y tierra
y Baba está por todos lados cuelga
sobre las vacas que duermen a la sombra
y los mendigos y las mujeres vestidas con telas celestes y rosas
vemos todo
como ciervos que corren por el campo abierto
y paran de golpe hay algo

traduce Susana

dice el señor
que antes el pueblo se llamaba
el hogar de pastores de vacas Gollapalli
que estaba todo el campo lleno de bellas vacas gordas
y un pastor
preocupado porque su favorita no le daba leche
la encontró amamantando a una cobra
se enfureció agarró una piedra aplastó a la cobra y ella
silbando su último suspiro
soltó una maldición ahora la tierra dijo
será un hormiguero

y el auto dobló
y cruzamos las puertas del ashram
los jardines
donde los dioses están quietos
es celeste su piel de mono su cabeza o de elefante
y los fieles vestidos con blanco panyabi
con una pequeña bandera atada al cuello
cantan om bajo los árboles en llamas
y esperan para a que empiece el darshan la visión de dios
donde aparece Baba

esos chicos
corren atrás del auto quieren bajar valijas
por unas rupias quieren
subirlas a este cuarto con dos camas dos colchones
que alquilamos en el ashram
van a hacer una excepción dice Susana
para que puedas dormir acá porque hombres y mujeres
    duermen
y comen y rezan separados
y yo
yo tendré que aprender
a comer con el silencio de las plantas
ceremoniosamente ir hasta el mandir
a pedirle a Sai Baba que cure a mi madre a pedir
con un grave fluir de silencio

Liliana
flor de lirio trae un coco
lleno de agua que dice te alimenta como un bife de vaca
y que ese hombre vende y corta con un machete

ahora yo
estoy vestido de blanco también
con una pequeña bandera argentina en la espalda
con un punto de ceniza entre los ojos
ceniza de bosta de vaca quemada con leche ceniza del
   cosmos vibhuti
mientras el sol se oculta y vela los caminos
y más atrás las colinas de Anantapur y el mar ceniciento y
   más atrás
mi propia casa
mi padre el labrador

3 a.m
suena la alarma
salgo en silencio no quiero
despertar a mi madre tan temprano
mientras el sueño anida en su cabeza todavía
y en la cabeza de los pájaros
conozco el camino hasta el templo y conozco a los dioses
quietos al borde del sendero como higueras
amarradas al mundo con raíces
en la casa de Baba no hay luces prendidas
está cerrado el locutorio la cantina donde como solo
los grillos
y este raro crujido de pisadas
machacan el silencio
y la distancia aunque ya somos varios
vestidos de blanco sentados en fila esperando a que abran
las puertas del mandir
y faltan horas
mi madre dice que madrugo
para que dios me escuche a mi primero
pero lo que me gusta es una pierna doblada sobre otra
este hormigueo adentro de las manos el brazo dormido
mientras los pájaros despiertan
y el día fosforece en todo
y todo es tan tranquilo que apenas sé por qué
estoy acá
una hormiga en la fila de hormigas
con el primer rayo de sol

abren las puertas

entramos al templo nos hacen cantar para llamar a dios

cinco om por la nariz ojos orejas piel y lengua

por los pies el ano el pene las manos la garganta

por el aire que vive en el cuerpo

por lo que envuelve al cuerpo

y un último om para mí mismo

shanti shanti shanti

esto es lo que habla cuando nadie habla

a qué suena
el cántaro de la cabeza
un arroyo de lluvia de canto de pájaros
esa ramita de sentido al borde de mi plato en la cantina
y si me muevo
y si me acerco a la corriente
es el seseo de las flores es la piedra que cae al agua
el nombre luminoso como un claro en el bosque de ruido
o más concretamente un estadounidense
que casi en castellano dice algo

esto es lo que habla cuando nadie habla

cuando el pie de mi madre
se torció por culpa de un montículo de tierra
nos tomamos un rickshaw ella mostró un tobillo hinchado
y el hombre nos trajo a la guardia
el salón está lleno
somos los únicos vestidos de blanco y la gente se acerca
parecen preocupados por mi madre
hablan en hindi en sánscrito en qué hablan
para ser este oráculo
que responde a una pregunta
que no me quiero hacer que nadie hizo

esto es lo que habla cuando nadie habla

estaba en el mandir
esperando a que saliera Baba el sol recién aparecía
y entonces un idioma que me hablaba
rugoso como la voz
de alguien que volviéndose un árbol tiene labios todavía
el viejo con la piel de ébano
sin bandera colgada en el cuello
inhaló un largo hilo de aire y exhaló un ovillo compacto sin
    resabios
y me miró como diciendo ahora es tu turno
olvidá lo que te trajo
tu escuela tus amigos la chica que te gusta tu otra vida

esto es lo que habla cuando nadie habla

y los dedos del día despiertan al cielo
lavan la niebla de sus párpados
y todos van hasta las puertas del templo quieren llegar
    primero
como un viento
cuando trae un murmullo de olas vestidas de blanco
que se levantan y corren a la playa
con la boca abierta

y ese mono bebé
mi hermana se acerca despacio
quiere tocar ese pelaje con sus propios dedos
ahora su madre mono sale de la nada aúlla le tira la ropa y
    el pelo
está furiosa ahora
bajan monos de los árboles
rodean a mi hermana

como lava
que encandila a un mono de la selva
así los fieles salen
cuando ven a dios

y el hombre que arma bolsas de ceniza
bajo el alero como el ala de un insecto
con una pala junta y llena cada bolsa
con ceniza del cosmos
bajo el ala de un insecto

como grillos que cantan a la noche
agazapados en la nada
en un campo de fuerza de sonido
así los mantras
por todas partes
como grillos

y qué diría
mi padre el labrador
si me viera sentado solo
comiendo arroz
vestido con panyabi blanco

como una jaula en el jardín de dios
esa higuera de bengala
con raíces aéreas en las ramas que crecen hacia abajo
se incrustan en la tierra
en el jardín de dios

y oí
el pájaro
que gira
arriba de un largo om
sus pequeñas garras de pájaro
lo van rasgando

como la araña
que le da vueltas a su presa
la envuelve con su tela así
el sastre rodea a mi madre con un sari
como la araña

metida en su caja de vidrio
la diosa me mira
con todas sus cabezas
una pegada a la otra sus cinco cabezas
me sigue con los ojos
abiertos mientras voy al templo
a las tres de la mañana

como hormigas negras
que siempre salen de la nada y cargan
las hojas errantes que el viento derrama
así los rickshaws salen y nos llevan
como hormigas

y esa mujer
que me ofreció
pedacitos marrones y blancos de coco
mientras paseaba solo por el ashram
cerca de la cascada
la mujer de los cocos

y los dioses están ahí mirándonos
y los dioses están ahí mirándonos

las lavanderas
que vi al trepar la colina
brillan vestidas de blanco en el valle lavando las sábanas
    blancas
en el agua que brilla
entre los campos verdes las colinas

todo el día
mi voz se quedó en mi garganta
como un ratón
que se metió en un mueble
un nudo de silencio en mi garganta

como fantasmas
esas ráfagas de diente y pelo
mis compañeras de la escuela
me masturbé pensando en ellas a la hora de la siesta
no las veo hace mucho y ahora
son estas ráfagas de diente y pelo

era de noche
y me senté en mi silla plegable
a esperar que las puertas del templo estuvieran abiertas
ahora es de día
canto para llamar a dios
y viene

la cabeza mojándose en el río
en este huerto lleno de frutales
de flores y pájaros sin nombre
las vacas tiradas a la sombra
y el Taunus de mi padre
recién lavado con el motor en marcha
será sagrada
la ceniza de bosta quemada en mi frente
la nave que cruza la noche
los dioses escondidos en el campo
el olor de las reses a la tarde en Mataderos
y mi madre
viniendo hacia mí como un perro una araña en otra vida
las cabezas de dios que me miran
Sai Baba vestido de naranja haciendo que aparezca algo
y la isla de Eolo
donde llegó Ulises donde nació mi abuelo
lavanderas que brillan en el valle con sus sábanas
y mi hermana con nueve años en panyabi blanco
y el mono que tira del pelo
será sagrado
el coco recién cortado
mi tía con sus ángeles
los taxis los mapas los chicos que suben valijas
los pasos de los dioses por el cielo
será sagrado
el cáncer de mi madre
esta estirpe de hojas que el viento derrama y devuelve
el humo del asado
las turbinas que suenan como estrellas

vuelta

Se terminó
debajo el avión nubes de humo
llegan de la tierra y entran a la casa de los dioses
donde el aire suena al viento y las estrellas
bajo más
la nave cruza el piso de las nubes
sobre el río las islas los arroyos que se meten por los campos
esta tierra boscosa despoblada si no fuera
porque está labrada
y porque el ruido sube y bajo más
y más presiona el aire en los oídos
el sonido condensado de este viaje de otra vida
porque ahora estoy en casa y el avión ya
toca tierra

Este libro se terminó de escribir el veinticuatro de enero de 2018.

Liliana flor de lirio murió el primero de noviembre de 2000.

Jorge el labrador murió el veintiocho de mayo de 2016.

Susana flor de loto sigue oyendo los pasos de los dioses en el cielo y compra ángeles en Once.

Acknowledgments

To my guides, Mirta Rosenberg and Florencia Montesano;
to Ezequiel Zaidenwerg and Alejandro Crotto for the gift of
   their reading and their friendship;
to Robin Myers for the extraordinary honor of her translation;
to Michelle Gil-Montero, Román Antopolsky, Bridget
   Fertal, and Tyler Friend of Eulalia Books;
to my sister Nadia,
thank you.

Thanks to *Tupelo Quarterly,* where "Susana, lotus flower,"
"Liliana, lily blossom," "Sai Baba," "I wake up in India,"
multiple fragments of "silence," and "is this what sacred
means?" previously appeared.

Translator's Note

Translation—like music or friendship or anything else we might pursue in the name of pleasure and curiosity—is a balance between intuition and effort. It's an interpolation (*this speaks to me*) followed by an ask (*how does it work?*).

In late 2018, when I first read *Otra vida*, Daniel Lipara's debut, I felt instant flares of affinity for its quiet, observant warmth. I admired its work with the autobiographical mode, its narrative centered on a family trip in which the adolescent speaker, his younger sister, his terminally ill mother, and his New-Age-enthusiast aunt travel from their middle-class, predominantly Jewish neighborhood in Buenos Aires to Sai Baba's ashram in Puttaparthi, India. I was struck by Lipara's use of Homeric epithets (e.g., "Liliana lily blossom," "Susana lotus flower," and "Jorge the tiller") as a gesture that gently honors his anti-heroes, his flawed beloveds. Finally, I was moved by the awakening documented in this poem (Lipara has described *Another Life* as one long poem in fifteen parts): a boy's initiations into the power of language, his poetic vocation, a more sweeping perception of his childhood, and his capacity for wonderment, all while orbiting an inexorable loss.

After this spontaneous rush of connection, I began to focus more deliberately on the poem's looping composition and expansive prosody. Lipara reaches forward and backward in space (Argentina, India, and Lipari Island), in time (from the fabled age of Aeolus, to the early lives of the speaker's parents, and to his own teenage years), and in the speaker's consciousness (which chronicles other "characters" or channels their voices, and which lands on a piercing coda that marks the dates of his parents' deaths and of the book's finish). *Another Life* is, in a way, an origin myth, and Lipara continually engages with Homer to explore, tease, and subvert the idea of the epic: from his use of epithets to his quiet transposition and reconfiguration of certain Iliadic episodes (think Hector and Andromache in the Buenos Aires airport) to the inevitable homecoming. But his cinematic arcs through space and time never feel grandiose in their scale. They're modest, unassuming, and somehow as organic as a tidal pull, an ebb and flow that never ceases to stream back into itself—a Möbius strip.

As I translated (and, more to the point, as I revised), I strived to protect the gesturality of this poem, which is both purposeful and free. Sentences are largely unpunctuated and uncapitalized. The diction is by turns as colloquial as speech, solemn as myth, and frank and rhythmic as prayer. Almost the entire book is in the present tense, whether the subject is the Roman Empire or Aunt Susana buying angel stickers in Buenos Aires. It doesn't serve to erase the distinction between present and past; it highlights how they forever fold into each other in a way that linear narrative cannot contain.

I steeped my English in a similar amalgam of present-tenseness; I too strived for a register that could shift between—or sift together—contemporary and ancient, cheeky and reverent, candid and oblique. For starters, I decided to translate in a loosely metered line, allowing myself to veer in and out of an iambic cadence. My intention was never to pursue a syllabic system, to assert and uphold a particular metrical form. But the iambic mode—a powerful bedrock under the English-language poetic history, and a resource still ripe for exploring and transgressing—allowed me a sense of rhythmic structure to follow and then intermittently intensify, dilute, or interrupt throughout the text. This approach engages with (without trying to directly mirror) Lipara's own: *Otra vida* observes, explores, adapts, and departs from various syllabic lines in the Spanish-language tradition. In both cases (with Lipara's approach being more syllabic at first and mine being more accentual), even a relaxed metrical structure somehow dapples the poem's contemporary appearance on the page. Or maybe it's the other way around—maybe it's the most visibly present-day dynamics at work in *Another Life* that run an electrical charge through its traditional underpinnings.

Lipara's original project directly engages with the work of two brilliant poet-translators, neither of whom I'd read before I encountered his book. When I did, hoping to learn more about where he had centered his attention, both of them became essential influences on my translation as well. The first is Emily Wilson and her magnificent translation of the *Odyssey* (2017). I was awed by her strong blank verse, clear diction, and vibrant epithets; her *Odyssey* helped to tune my ear for Lipara's Homeric tribute. The second is Alice Oswald and her harrowing *Memorial*, a poetic "excavation" of the *Iliad* that commemorates every soldier killed in that epic, juxtaposed with a chorus of Homeric similes. *Memorial* (a book Lipara himself translated into Spanish with his friend and mentor, the late Argentine poet and publisher Mirta Rosenberg) alerted me to the possibility of surging rhythms in poems that seem stark at first glance. It helped me find richness in the spare.

Now a confession. I'm revising this brief essay on a flight back to Mexico, where I live, after traveling to see my parents for the first time since the Covid-19 pandemic began. As naïve as it sounds, I've been feeling newly thunderstruck by the fact—does it really ever sink in?—that we live only once, and not for very long; that we can't exist in more than one place at a time; that we can't remember everything we experience; that we are bound to lose what we love and be changed by both (loss, love). I keep thinking of a passage from this book:

I'm eleven
I'm drinking orange juice with my mother in a coffee shop
I think I won't remember her
won't recognize her if I see her in another life
don't be like that souls travel as a group yes even in the stars
they change I might become your grandson or your cousin
   imagine that
a dog you have a spider in its web
a flower blooming on the terrace

The spider later returns ("my mother / coming toward me like a dog a spider in another life"), an image that leaves me shaken every time. It's connected to what moves me most about *Another Life*: the notion that we can't possibly know where our history begins, along with the promise that loss implies transformation. Is this what sacred means? the speaker asks toward the end.

I'm inexpressibly grateful to Daniel for his company, generosity, and trust throughout the translation process, and for our conversations since. His book grows both more familiar and more mysterious to me over time. The combination is itself a kind of miracle, I think, as friendship is.

Robin Myers
June 2021